Six-Word Lessons on

# THE SPORT OF RUNNING

100 Lessons to Enjoy
Running for a Lifetime

## Tracey Cohen

Published by Pacelli Publishing
Bellevue, Washington

"I loved Tracey's book. With concise focus on all that is important for all runners, Tracey emphasizes the plus factors, such as how to enjoy life to the fullest, make friends and live life well through this simple activity of running. Tracey also makes the essential nuts and bolts facts clear. This book is essential for all those who don't believe in themselves and never thought they were athletes. Tracey's book offers everyone a start to find new, happier lives."

-- ***Bill Rodgers***, Four-time winner of the New York City and Boston Marathons, 1975-1980, Member of U.S. Olympic Team, 1976, Author of *Marathon Man*

"With wit, freshness, and vision, Tracey has beautifully captured the essence of the sport of distance running in 100 valuable lessons. Each lesson's title is condensed to six words, leading the reader to a nugget of wisdom drawn from Tracey's extensive experience as a distance runner. When combined, these 100 nuggets of wisdom form a gold mine of information, guidance, and inspiration that will benefit runners of all ages, motives, and abilities. Her book is a tour de force of running's many facets, from shoe/clothing selection to training tips, nutrition to injuries, and running safety to the runner's psyche. Runners will find the chapter on accredited running organizations and trusted resources especially helpful. Just as every runner is different, every runner will find value in Tracey's exploration of distance running as not just a sport, but a personal journey in achieving both physical and mental health through this unique human activity known as running."

--**_Mitchell Garner_**, President of Road Runners Club of America and Ann Arbor Track Club

# Six-Word Lessons on
# the Sport of Running

Published by Pacelli Publishing
9905 Lake Washington Blvd. NE, #D-103
Bellevue, Washington 98004
PacelliPublishing.com

Cover and interior design by Pacelli Publishing

ISBN-10: 1-933750-63-4
ISBN-13: 978-1-933750-63-7

# Contents

# Author's Note

While this book is not intended to be a complete source of running nor am I a complete authority on our sport, I do hope that runners - beginning, advanced and everywhere in between - will find value in my words and running career, now in its thirty-third consecutive year.

Just as you will find a great deal of information in the pages ahead for the beginning runner, it is also my goal to offer a fresh perspective that will encourage every runner to breathe new life into your training and racing; offer comfort, support and inspiration; provide motivation for those on hiatus to return to our wonderful sport; and welcome one and all to enjoy running in whatever way suits you best.

Thank you for choosing to explore my point of view; I can't wait to celebrate with you on the glorious roads, tracks and trails just waiting to be explored.

*Tracey*

# Acknowledgements

I would like thank Maureen Burry, the hospital childcare worker who introduced running and, in effect, a lifeline, to a very scared, confused and misunderstood preteen trying to make sense of a world so very foreign to my true nature.

To the running community at large (as there are just too many of you to single out with individual names), I bestow my sincere gratitude and appreciation to each and every individual who welcomed me in from the very beginning and has continued to accept me, quirks and all.

Finally, I would be remiss if I did not recognize and thank my incredible publishers, Patty and Lonnie Pacelli, whose patience, generosity, kindness, support and brilliance have been invaluable from the very beginning.

I am so very grateful to have each and every one of you in my life.

# Jogger or Runner? It's Your Decision.

# 1

# An "entry blank" makes the difference.

Noted physician, author and *Runner's World* editor, Dr. George A. Sheehan believed, "The difference between a jogger and a runner is an entry blank." Like Sheehan, for many, the art of racing and becoming a stronger, faster, improved athlete is the real purpose of running.

2

# Synonyms which bear very different connotations

Runners typically strive to be trained athletes. They take pride in their dedication, consistency and efforts to improve pace, strength and endurance. Alternatively, joggers generally enjoy a more casual approach, placing greater emphasis on the social component and calories burned than the quality and frequency of their runs.

3

# Speed a runner does not make.

Not all runners are elite and the elite are not all runners. Pace alone does not distinguish a runner or jogger. It's the will and dedication to train and compete; to share your craft and passion; to experience and learn; to be the student and the teacher. Speed will come and go, but authentic passion is what makes a true runner.

# 4

# Runners run thoughtfully with off days.

Mindful of form, frequency and pace, we run long, short, in between and some days not at all. Non-running days are used to cross train or rest completely dependent on bodily needs. Routes and running surfaces are varied; complacency and predictability are to be avoided which often lead to poor form, lethargy and injury.

# 5

# We find the time and motivation.

Too hot, too cold, busy schedule, just don't wanna. Internal and external circumstances challenge even the most dedicated, but runners create opportunities, seeking and finding inspiration on the dreariest of days. And on the occasions we fall short, guilt-ridden and envious, we are reminded of the beauty in every run leaving us determined and re-energized.

# 6

# Are runners destined for more fun?

In the 1992 film, *A League of Their Own,* Tom Hanks' character Jimmy Dugan insisted, "If it wasn't hard, everyone would do it. The hard . . . is what makes it great." Greater investment produces greater emotional response, reaping rewards and risking disappointments. I find euphoric success and heartbreaking disappointment versus general indifference to be more "fun" every time.

# 7

# Am I a real runner yet?

There is no judge, jury or authority to discipline imposters and determine runner versus jogger. However, if you beg the question and desire the reputation, you likely have achieved runner status – an athlete who trains consistently, seeks information about the sport, enters races and cares about performance. If this is you then I do believe you have emerged!

# 8

# Run or jog, it's all good.

Incorporating the sport of running into life on an individual level is important and will keep you coming back for more. Whether you jog or run, roads, trails and tracks don't discriminate. They're ready when we are. Honor thy body, appreciate each jaunt, value the ability to enjoy and reap the benefits of such an inclusive, multidimensional sport.

# 9

# Just enjoy running; labels are overrated.

Passion should not and cannot be forced. Running can be incorporated as an important component in maintaining fitness, training for other disciplines and taking part in social events. Better to find value using a less disciplined approach than loathe and resent an integral sport intended to evoke positive physical and emotional results.

# Shoes Matter – Your Most Important Equipment

# 10

# Every runner needs a good shoe.

Quality footwear is necessary for runners of every level and ability – fast and slow; high mileage and low; consistent and intermittent. Setting up for success is important, initial intentions and abilities notwithstanding. Happy feet can only benefit body and mind, enhancing the journey and likelihood of reaching and even surpassing individual goals.

# 11

# Best practices for buying running shoes

Run specialty stores pride themselves on carrying quality footwear and ensuring the proper fit for each individual consumer. Personal history is considered, foot and gait analyzed before educated staff make recommendations to support customer needs and goals. Throughout the fit process, size, width and feel are checked for comfort, function and support.

# 12

# Support your arch type and gait.

Before choosing a shoe, it is important to determine the foot's arch strength and height. While there is no definitive rule, stability shoes generally work best for medium to low arches that collapse when bearing weight, commonly referred to as over-pronation. Neutral cushioned shoes tend to work well for medium to high arches that do not fall under pressure.

# 13

# Running shoes built for different purposes

There are many running footwear choices. While there are no rules, generally use lightweight shoes for speed work and racing. Supportive shoes are best for the bulk of training, and use spikes for track races. Trail shoes are for off-road terrain, and waterproof shoes are for wet and extreme cold. Being an informed consumer is important in determining what will best suit personal needs and desires.

# 14

# The implications of running shoe prices

Price alone does not determine superiority, but better, longer lasting materials used in choice shoe models cost more than inferior counterparts. Newer shoe models generally require more research and advertising for fewer units produced, so they are more expensive. I don't advise sacrificing quality for lower prices, and it's always valuable to stay current on the latest information.

# 15

# Favored shoe models will update regularly.

Manufacturers routinely revamp shoe models. Because individual feet and preferences vary, changes will benefit some while alienating others. Therefore, it is best to try various brands and models in addition to trending, recommended and favorite products. The only "best" shoe is subject to each person's unique foot shape, gait, preference and budget, which can change over time.

# 16

# Replace your shoes: when and why

It's important to retire running shoes once the support structure deteriorates. Shoes may look fine, but often the built-in support is not. Replace your lifeless feeling shoes before body aches begin and develop into injury. Rotating footwear, staggering usage and start dates, can extend shoe longevity and better determine when to replace them.

# 17

# Why such fuss over shoe selection?

Proper footwear helps keep the body in neutral alignment and cushions the impact of running. Benefits include decreased risk of injury, longevity in the sport and maximized enjoyment. Likewise, the right fit will decrease the chance of blisters, bunions, nerve damage and other problems that can be caused by ill-fitting footwear.

# Running Myths: They're Just not True.

# 18

# Running is bad for your knees.

Excessive body weight, over-pronation, weak, tight, imbalanced muscles, unsupportive footwear, poor form, improper training and poor nutrition are all harmful to the knees. Because running is weight-bearing, it helps strengthen bones, ligaments and joints. The right approach, along with modifications as needed, will allow for strong, injury-free running long into your twilight years.

# 19

# Stretching before a run causes injury.

A proper warmup and cooldown will help keep muscles loose, balanced and injury free. Pre-run dynamic stretches will safely release muscle tension and increase blood flow, whereas static stretches are better reserved for post-run flexibility and increased range of motion.

20

# Running alone provides sufficient strength training.

While running strengthens major leg, hip and gluteal muscles, you also need strong abdominal, shoulder, back, and arm muscles, especially as the body tires, to maintain good form and avoid muscle imbalances and injury. Doing simple run-specific strength exercises a few times a week can accomplish this task and improve running performance.

# 21

# Shoe weight directly affects running performance.

Lightweight footwear may add confidence and shave some seconds off running performance results. However, be mindful that ill-fitting, unsupportive footwear can lead to injury. Comfortable running shoes customized to individual needs will feel light and enhance performance more than actual decreased shoe weight. A balance between the two is ideal.

# 22

# Carbo-load the night before a race.

While eating a carbohydrate rich pre-race meal prior to race day can have its benefits, effective carbo-loading and proper nutrition should happen weeks in advance. A large meal high in carbo-hydrates is more likely to leave you bloated and full than prove beneficial. Instead, eat a modest, familiar, proportionate meal for peak performance.

# 23

# It's just a 5K; that's easy.

There are some who perpetuate the illusion that running and racing farther is better and harder. Anyone can slog out more miles. It is the quality of a run that makes it great and challenging. Develop your individual distance, terrain and speed goals and be assured that your personal aspirations are as worthy as the next.

24

# Running is tedious, lonely and one-dimensional.

Run short, far, solo, on a team or with friends on road, track, grass or trail. Speed up, slow down; race, socialize, and improve fitness. Run to raise charitable funds or to simply enjoy its inherent movement. Running can be simplistic or strategic, and be combined with other disciplines. Athletes evolve and taper to suit their individual needs and desires.

## 25

# I'm too old to start running!

Running can be enjoyed by everyone; requirements include a willingness to put one foot in front of the other and ideally, a sound pair of shoes. Pace, goals, form and running surfaces can all be learned and adjusted to each individual's needs, desires and changing life circumstances. It's never too late to begin, revisit or redesign your running career.

26

# Personal records become unattainable with age.

Our bodies change as we mature, and so can our mental and physical approach. Healthy nourishment and adjustments to training programs, race strategies and personal goals will allow for continued quality running and peak performances. Relish the ability to reinvent yourself; enjoy new challenges, establish new goals, employ a fresh approach relevant to your current versus former self.

# Other Beneficial Equipment and Fun Stuff

# 27

# Materials that perform better than cotton

Wools and synthetics pull moisture away from the body and are highly permeable. These features are essential for maintaining ideal body temperatures and avoiding blisters and chafing. Clothing with these attributes is most important for socks and other garments in direct contact with the skin. Running stores, experienced runners and product reviews can provide trusted information when choosing specific brands and models.

# 28

# Runners must see and be seen.

Headlamps and hand torches, many designed specifically for running, provide ample lighting for running in poor visibility and dark conditions. They also make runners conspicuous to oncoming foot and vehicular traffic. Reflective vests, bands, stickers and tape, clip on lights and shoes, apparel and hats with built in reflective properties also increase visibility.

## 29

# The benefits of wearing compression gear

Graduated compression can improve circulation by helping muscles loosen up faster and stay warm, leaving the body less prone to fatigue and injury. Compression socks and sleeves are most common, but shorts, tights, tops and braces are also available. Though compression will not cure an injury, it can lend support on the run and during the healing process.

# 30

# Benefits of watches and fitness trackers

Running watches and fitness trackers can complement your training by offering a wide range of functions, including the ability to record time, distance, speed, heart rate, stride length and calories burned. Increased performance, motivation and fitness can result. I encourage runners to also run naturally without the use of external devices to facilitate access to valuable intrinsic information.

# 31

# Ouch! Nobody likes blisters or chafing.

A few top products for runners that safeguard against chafing and blisters in convenient, no-mess formulas and packaging include Body Glide LLC.'s anti-chafe sticks that glide on easily and protect vulnerable areas of the body; RunGuards LLC.'s unique NipGuards® specifically protect our nipples, and Medi-Dyne's 2TOMS brand BlisterShield® powders take care of our feet.

# 32

# Carry essential possessions on the run.

Nathan, Amphipod and Ultimate Direction are a few prominent companies that design run-specific packs, belts and carriers for identification, hydration and other personal effects. I encourage athletes to balance need and desire so as not to compromise running integrity and quality with excessive, cumbersome belongings.

# 33

# Fuel the body on the run.

Convenient and easily digestible, a vast array of pre-packaged gels, chews, beans, bites, bars and hydration products, in powdered, tablet and ready-to-drink form, are available to replenish the body's nutrients before, during and after a run. Reputed companies, including GU Energy, CLIF and Hammer Nutrition, create numerous options to keep you nourished and hydrated.

# 34

# Jogging strollers for children and pets

With permission from your pediatrician or veterinarian, running with children and pets can be safe and enjoyable on pavement and trails. BOB and Pet Gear Inc. are two proven jogging stroller manufacturers whose products allow parents and caretakers to share their running with children and pets who can't run on their own or need a push along the way.

# 35

# Weather resistant head and neck wear

Balaclavas and similar multifunctional head and neckwear are wonderful assets for regulating body temperature in every kind of weather. Available in various moisture wicking fabrics and styles, BUFF®, along with other reputable companies, manufactures seemingly simple pieces of cloth which can be used to combat perspiration and act as a barrier against wind, cold and harmful ultraviolet rays.

# 36

# Footwear traction for ice and snow

Outfit running shoes with traction to ensure safe, slip-free running during frosty winter conditions. Due North, Kahtoola and Yak Trax are reputable manufacturers that produce slip-on and slip-off footwear devices with spikes and other nonslip equivalents. Icespike products screw spikes directly into the shoe sole, and some companies produce footwear equipped with traction specific for icy conditions.

## 37

# Snowshoes add excitement to winter running.

By evenly spreading an individual's weight across their oversized, flat surface, snowshoes allow athletes to move through the snow without sinking. Run-specific snowshoes, narrower and lighter than traditional models, are best for running and racing. With minor tweaks in form, beginners and veterans alike can enjoy recreational or competitive snowshoe running throughout the cold winter months.

# Accredited Running Organizations and Trusted Resources

# 38

# The Road Runners Club of America

Since 1958, RRCA has remained committed to the "development of community-based running clubs and events that serve runners of all ages and abilities in pursuit of health and competition." RRCA provides resources needed for long-term success including insurance protection, event assistance, innovative programs and education on all things running – all of which benefit member clubs and individual runners.

39

# USATF drives competitive excellence, popular engagement.

USA Track & Field is the governing body for track and field, long-distance running and race walking in the U.S. They sanction events, certify courses, establish and enforce regulations, create and promote grassroots programs and member organizations. USATF creates opportunities for athletes of all ages and abilities.

40

# A network geared for masters athletes

USATF Masters (USATF.org) and USA Masters Track & Field are devoted to providing information and healthy, competitive opportunities specific to masters athletes thirty years and older in track and field and race walking, and forty years and older in long distance running. Any and all experience, interest and ability levels are encouraged and supported.

41

# *Runner's World* has something for everyone.

Since 1966, *Runner's World* magazine has endeavored to improve the lives of every runner by providing information on training, nutrition, injury prevention, and motivational stories. No longer just a magazine, *Runner's World* has evolved into a brand, a "one-stop source for anything running-related" through its website, social media venues, events, books and international publications.

## 42

# *Trail Runner* – for off-road running devotees.

For those who like to get a little dirty and experience the beauty and often technical challenge of trail running, *Trail Runner* is committed to providing inspiration and up-to-date professional information on gear, training and racing for all levels of runners through its magazine, website, digital newsletter and social media venues.

# 43

# Passion for running beyond 26.2 miles

"The voice of the sport" since 1981, *UltraRunning* magazine has been a reliable source of up-to-date information for long distance runners, especially those looking to challenge themselves beyond the marathon distance. Content inspired by and for experienced and amateur athletes alike is provided on gear, races, interviews, training, nutrition and tangible enthusiasm for the sport as a whole.

## 44

# Running USA – our sport's trade organization

Since 1999, Running USA, a nonprofit organization established to benefit the running industry, has worked to advance the sport of running by promoting cohesive efforts of everyone in the sport. The heart of their work includes educational initiatives, industry research, networking opportunities, events and positive media relations.

45

# Girls on the Run inspires girls.

A 501(c)3 nonprofit organization, Girls on the Run teaches life skills to girls and incorporates running as an integral part of the curriculum. Educated coaches and volunteers motivate girls to be joyful, healthy and confident as the girls are coached to complete a 5K run and provided the foundation to "learn, dream, live, run" for generations to come.

46

# Medals4Mettle supports another kind of race.

A nonprofit organization near and dear to my heart, Medals4Mettle collects hard earned marathon, half marathon and triathlon medals from runners around the world to honor children and adults fighting debilitating illnesses. These medals, attached to a Medals4Mettle branded ribbon, are gifted to patients in recognition of the mettle and courage displayed in their race to continue living.

47

# Blind and visually impaired athletes run!

United States Association of Blind Athletes, United in Stride and Running Blind are three of many nonprofit organizations committed to providing athletic opportunities for all people with visual impairment. Among their many services, these organizations match trained guides with visually impaired athletes, which is essential for their ability to train, race and achieve life-altering goals in the process.

48

# Discover, explore and utilize local resources.

Running clubs, races, speakers, group runs and training programs found within your community are great assets and wonderful ways to connect with like-minded athletes, who often have a wealth of information and experience to share. To create your own group, RRCA (RRCA.org) and USATF (USATF.org) both offer guidance and tools for club leaders, event directors, coaches and runners.

# Maintenance Techniques for Prolonged Healthy Running

## 49

# Flexibility and strength must be earned.

Develop, incorporate and modify a strength and flexibility program relevant to your individual goals and needs so you can enhance and prolong your running endeavors. Never a one size fits all task, consultation with an experienced, trusted coach can help assess and determine your needs and transform weaknesses into strengths, making you a more complete runner.

50

# Release muscle tightness and trigger points.

Self-massage can help keep muscles loose and release fascia trigger points, knots that form in muscles. Foam rollers, massage sticks and lacrosse balls are a few of the many products available in addition to your own hands, to help relieve tension and allow muscles to return to a more pliable, active condition.

# 51

# The benefits of professional therapeutic massage

Trained therapists with vast knowledge of the body's anatomy can often better detect muscle tension and trigger points which fester in areas of the body that are hard to locate and reach. Increased relaxation and surreal ambiance are often additional benefits. A balance of professional massage and self-maintenance can help preserve optimal physical health for years.

## 52

# Fascial Stretch Therapy® focuses on fascia

Fascial Stretch Therapy® is a technique used to increase the range of motion in a joint by spotlighting and loosening the fascia, the most prevalent connective tissue in the body, which in turn increases muscle pliability. Functional assessments are implemented to customize treatment for each individual athlete. Certified Fascial Stretch Therapy® practitioners can be found at StretchtoWin.com.

# 53

# Comprehensive training enhances body and mind.

Create and sustain diverse training regimens including a variety of running drills, routes and strength exercises. A challenging mix will help offset the repetitive nature of running; reduce risk of injury; improve performance; increase motivation and enjoyment; and build a physical and mental toughness that will transcend the race course and filter through your everyday life.

## 54

# Seek knowledge, inspiration and fresh tactics.

Reading publications, attending speaker events, volunteering, attending races as a spectator or participant and chatting and running with other runners are invaluable opportunities to absorb worthwhile information and motivation. No matter your age, talent or level of experience, there is always more to learn and inspiration to gain from both beginning and experienced runners.

# 55

# Regular icing can promote faster recovery.

Professional opinions will vary, but I find that cold therapy as a preventative measure helps keep inflammation and muscle soreness to a minimum and reduces injury risk. Some swelling and discomfort is to be expected, especially when we push our bodies to the extreme, but generous, diligent upkeep helps avoid excessive, unwanted effects.

# 56

# Drink water liberally, purposefully and often.

Water is vital for digestion, regulating body temperature, building muscle, preventing cramps and strains, and lubricating tissues and joints. While too much water can push the body's electrolytes outside safe limits, the importance of ample hydration for athletic performance, recovery and sustenance of life should not be minimized or ignored. Clear, pale urine is one indicator of proper hydration.

# 57

# Nourish, respect and love your body.

We demand a lot from body and mind; in turn, we must feed heart and soul with consistent tranquil sleep, wholesome nutrition and quality rest days. Define and refine your self-care to your personal needs and changing circumstances. The better we treat our bodies, the better we feel and perform as runners and in life as a whole.

# Injury. Don't Freak Out. Try This.

# 58

# REST is a
# four letter word.

Rest can take on different forms dependent on individual need. From no running or any form of physical exercise to a reduction in weekly mileage and intensity or something in between that may incorporate cross training, allow rest to be a friend versus foe. Your body will thank you.

59

# Past proven tactics may need fine-tuning.

Injury can be a symptom that training practices need to be re-examined, even those practices that have traditionally shown positive results. Whether it is a beloved shoe model that no longer provides ample support, total weekly mileage in need of downsizing or any similar instigator, take charge, make adjustments and return to blissful, worry-free running.

# 60

# Poor running mechanics can cause injury.

While few people naturally inherit ideal running form, our bodies have an amazing ability to adapt. Sometimes though, years of poor form can cause our bodies to break down. A trained professional can help to assess your form and determine if adjustments need to be made.

# 61

# Establish trust with a trained professional.

Avoid wasteful trial-and-error healing approaches and utilize instead an educated line of attack that will minimize your recovery path. If you are emotionally vulnerable and in distress, impartial guidance from a familiar, well-informed practitioner sympathetic to the plight of a runner is invaluable.

# 62

# We have choices when seeking help.

Sports medicine doctors can diagnose and treat many injuries and refer a specialist if needed. Alternatively, chiropractors, podiatrists, certified personal trainers and massage and fascial stretch therapists are also viable options depending on the nature and severity of the problem. Many clinics offer free injury assessments and trusted members of the running community can also offer valuable guidance.

# 63

# Stop running? Get a second opinion.

Professionals practice their trade, but nobody, no matter how clever, knows everything, nor do all patients' injuries respond to the same treatment. If you don't find success from the help you seek, no matter how esteemed their reputation, try, try again. Seek another opinion, ideally one who treats each individual with a fresh approach.

# 64

# Use injury as a learning tool.

Albert Einstein said, "Insanity is doing the same thing over and over again and expecting different results." Use good sense. Find the catalyst of your pain, and take proper measures to steer clear of another occurrence. Keep persevering, and embrace methods, even with modified frequency, that will allow healing.

65

# Patience. Stay the course. Have faith.

Running restrictions can leave a deceptive, detrimental weight on your mind and body that defy and cloud your logic. Be aware that minor setbacks are natural over the course of recovery. A designated treatment approach will shorten healing time, but risky, random on-again off-again attempts to resume preferred training goals could lead to further injury.

# 66

## Check your attitude. Eliminate negativity completely.

This is difficult for sure, but a worthy and possible goal. Use your energies and mental prowess to transform distress into a liberating experience. Allow a day to grieve and then get rid of all self-pity. Use time normally spent running to volunteer, cross-train, read, rest, or rejuvenate. The mind is a very powerful force; make the most of it.

# My Ten
# Commandments for
# Safe Running

# 67

# The best defense is good offense.

It's deplorable, but human predators do lurk in society, sometimes when least expected. Avoid being a target – stay tuned into the environment, make eye contact, and keep running routes varied and unpredictable. If music is a necessity, keep the volume low. Keep vulnerability to a minimum by exuding awareness, confidence and strength.

# 68

# Be visible morning, noon and night.

A wide array of reflective gear is available to keep you visible while running in dark, cloudy, or foggy conditions, including headlamps and other lightweight, compact lights. Additionally, no matter what time of day, always run on the left side of the road facing oncoming traffic. Remember – you are responsible for your own safety. Make the effort, don't become a statistic.

# 69

# Important precautions running in the heat

Light colored clothing and caps with wicking properties deflect the sun's rays and equip the body to stay dryer and cooler. Frequent, consistent hydration is especially important in warmer temperatures to balance water loss in the body. Drink liberally throughout the day as well as during and after each run. Hydration belts, handhelds and packs are recommended.

# 70

# Stay warm running in the cold.

Dressing in layers and covering extremities – head, ears, feet and hands, is essential for maintaining core body temperature in wintry conditions while not overheating. Moisture-wicking materials are recommended. Cotton absorbs sweat, leaving skin damp, while synthetics and wools pull moisture away, keeping the body dry and fresh.

# 71

# Sleet, snow, ice? Bring it on!

Challenging weather that slickens outdoor surfaces does not have to keep you from running outside, but do take precautions. Traction devices worn over shoes are available to help keep you upright. Adjust your pace and focus on surface conditions, being especially mindful of vehicular traffic.

# 72

# Favored methods to diffuse canine encounters

Even friendly, well trained dogs can become agitated and defensive by unfamiliar advancing targets. Remain as unthreatening as possible. Avoid eye contact, and give wide berths to dogs and their territory. Carry small stones to pretend-throw should a dog advance. If this doesn't help, throw the stone to scare only. Shrill whistles, squirt guns and dog treats can also help.

## 73

# Sound, respectful running with canine companions

Consult a veterinarian regarding the benefits and risks of running with your dog. Be sensitive to temperament, and distinguish the dog's enjoyable experiences versus its desire to please. Leashes are important for the wellbeing of everyone. All animals, no matter how well-trained or mild in disposition, are subject to inherent instincts, distracted drivers and those fearful of even the gentlest creatures.

74

# Everlasting, enjoyable running for every child

Expose kids of all ages and abilities to running in a fun, relaxed environment. Equip these budding athletes with proper footwear, opportunity and sound training. Your community, along with school fun runs and teams provide added motivation and resources for developing friendships, confidence, work ethic, healthy lifestyles, talent and drive.

75

# Tune in to your body's needs.

Listen closely and you will hear your body communicate. Learn to differentiate between the well-earned sweet aches of a hard, healthy workout and pain twinges – warnings that the body is overtaxed, experiencing muscle imbalances or in need of more rest. Heed bodily warnings and make training modifications as needed to gain long-lasting dividends and avoid extended layoffs.

76

# Strive for ideal, work within capacity.

Temper desire and information from trustworthy sources with overall physical condition. By respecting our bodies throughout decision-making processes regarding nutrition, training, racing, shoe choice and dressing for the weather, we can more easily avoid calamity. Set courageous goals while running responsibly for yourself, your support system and the running community at large.

# Pace, Time, Frequency and Running Surfaces

# 77

# Natural surfaces provide softer running alternatives.

Running on organic terrain such as grass, dirt, trail and gravel can decrease impact and strain on the body and provide a more scenic, tranquil experience. Due though to their uneven, inconsistent nature, be extra careful of foot placement to avoid trips and falls, and your pace should generally be slower proportionate to the intricacy of the course.

# 78

# Things to know about treadmill running

Treadmills offer a smooth, shock absorbent surface in a controlled environment, and are a good tool for fitness and recovery. However, to enjoy the pleasures and challenges of running outside, you'll need a gentle transition from the treadmill, along with proper outdoor gear.

## 79

# Tracks present advantages and stumbling blocks.

Synthetic tracks found in schools and gyms provide a soft, smooth, standardized running surface and distance, typically 200m and 400m, respectively, for indoor and outdoor tracks. While they are wonderful tools for speedwork, potential challenges include boredom, accessibility, cost and excessive physical stress from the track's long continuous curves. To reduce any risk of injury, change direction as allowed.

# 80

# Run faster to improve performance pace.

Speedwork is an important ingredient to incorporate during weekly training for the ability to run faster, longer. Strides, fartleks, and interval training as well as tempo and threshold runs are wonderful training techniques that can be crafted and further refined to suit each athlete's individual ability, progression, goals and circumstances.

# 81

# Respect the distance and be prepared.

Whether running competitively or casually, it is important to understand, train for and appreciate the duration you wish to run. More preparation is needed for factors such as weather, nutrition and hydration the longer you need to endure. Think less about, "Can I finish?" and more about, "Am I prepared to finish safely, responsibly and respectably?"

# 82

# Pace may not reflect effort exerted.

Terrain difficulty, weather conditions and route complexity can all affect speed. Embrace challenging circumstances, modify pace expectations and focus on quality of expended effort. The physical and mental advantages gained will provide strength when coping with life's unpredictable race and everyday conditions and build a faster, tougher, more well-rounded athlete.

## 83

# Forget the mileage, run for time.

As much value as there is in knowing pace and mileage, it's also important to run free of performance expectation pressures. Regularly schedule a run for time versus distance. Explore new routes, determine pace by feel, experience and value the privilege of putting one foot in front of the other simply because you can.

# 84

# Consistency trumps a daily running streak.

While there are some who pride themselves on running daily without deviation, this does not necessarily make for a stronger, healthier, faster, happier, motivated runner. Develop a schedule that jibes with current goals and stay consistent; allow modifications based on need versus unfounded excuses. Push through challenging situations but adjust when critical, non-negotiable circumstances must dictate.

# Oh the Races
# We can Run!

# 85

# The dessert after a well-balanced meal

Races add further value and accountability to running and proper training. They offer a tangible goal to be achieved in a competitive while supportive, festive environment. Race against the clock, other runners or solely within yourself. Good preparation increases your chance of achieving goals and enhancing the celebratory part of athletic endeavors.

# 86

# Road races come in many forms.

There are countless road races of nearly every imaginable distance for athletes to experience, test and hone their skills. Out and back, point to point, one big loop or multiple if desired, with fantastic quirky courses, runners will traverse neighborhoods, parks, bridges, tunnels, bike paths, country roads and even freeways closed to traffic! Envision the extraordinary; destiny awaits.

87

# Trail and mountain races venture off-road.

Scenic and unpretentious, with distances ranging from a few miles to hundreds of miles, off-road racing provides serene, beautiful venues with varying course intricacy levels that redefine speed and dramatically emphasize the natural beauty bestowed upon our earth. Dirt, sand, roots, mud, hills and stream crossings are a few of the more challenging elements runners may encounter.

# 88

# The sport of track and field

Held on an oval track that surrounds a grassy field, track and field competitions incorporate opportunities for athletes to run, jump, and throw. Sprints, hurdles, relays and middle and long distance comprise the running events. Shot put, hammer, discus and javelin make up the throwing contests, while long jump, triple jump, high jump and pole vault define the jump categories.

# 89

# Why choose a USATF certified course?

USA Track & Field established its course certification program to ensure the accuracy of measured distances for race courses. Competing on certified courses of equivalent distances allows for accurate comparison of timed perform-ances. In addition, only race times that are run on certified courses qualify for national rankings and record-setting.

## 90

# Marathon: 26 miles and 385 yards

In running lingo, the word marathon signifies 26.2 miles, typically in reference to a race. Courses will vary from road to trail, flat to mountainous, smooth to rugged, but the common denominator in every marathon, regardless of the number of competitors, is its total sum distance of 42 kilometers.

# 91

# Ultramarathons and stage races redefine endurance.

Ultramarathon races travel beyond the standard marathon distance. Stage races also exceed marathon distance but are divided into several stages accomplished over multiple days. Similarly, many ultramarathons exceed twenty-four hours, but they are run in a single stage. Terrain for both types of races will vary, and mileage generally ranges from 50 kilometers to hundreds of miles.

# 92

# Triathlons, duathlons, adventure and obstacle races

Multidiscipline race opportunities complement the run with at least one additional sport, including but not limited to, biking, swimming, trekking, canoeing, kayaking and orienteering. Training to perform at a high level for multiple sports simultaneously can keep motivation high and build a strong, passionate, all-round athlete.

# 93

# Time stipulated races offer another approach.

The goal in many races is to run a predetermined distance as quickly as possible. Timed races flip-flop the format, challenging athletes to run as many miles achievable in an allotted amount of time. Race courses are typically organized in a loop or out-and-back design, and competitions can range from one hour to seventy-two hours and beyond.

94

# Headstarts help to neutralize the competition.

Races that use a handicap age start system based on age and gender create a fun, tortoise and hare like atmosphere. By requiring runners to chase down competitors who have been given a head start, all athletes compete together in a more balanced format.

## 95

# Virtual races offer flexibility and convenience.

A virtual race is a self-timed event that can be run anywhere. In exchange for a registration fee, participants share their results and experience online or by mail and receive swag which typically includes a finisher's medal and sometimes a race bib and shirt. Virtual races may be connected with a physical race, and many support charitable organizations.

# 96

# Races are intended for kids too!

Many events allow children to race alongside adults while others are designed specifically for kids, including those in their very early years. From tot trots to modified multidiscipline affairs, races may include official finish times and age division awards, a sole finish line and participation awards, or any combination.

97

# Free for all
# Fat Ass races!

Fat Ass races are an ultrarunning tradition. These races may be completely unsupported without any course markings, aid, time clock or awards, or they may be a more conventional event. Some Fat Ass races ask participants to bring a nutrition item to share in lieu of an entry fee, and any awards are generally homemade or donated by participants and local businesses.

98

# A race within a race series

Some race directors create race series which present additional opportunities for competition and recognition in a friendly, motivating environment. Through participation in select races, runners also compete and accumulate points in the series based on performance, participation or both. While payment for the individual races is required, joining the race series is typically free of charge.

## 99

# Treat race organizers with tremendous respect.

Race directors and their crews, many of whom are volunteers, work tirelessly to put on quality and often charitable events that meet the needs of many diverse athletes. Post-race, always thank race personnel, and if desired, offer constructive feedback, after reflection and considering perspective. Bear in mind that slander in any form is unacceptable.

# 100

# How do I find race information?

Running clubs and run specialty stores stay current on race happenings as well as run-specific news and websites, many of which have race calendars. Two such examples include Active.com and RunningintheUSA.com. Ask questions, run a race or two and soon you will find yourself very much in the loop with numerous opportunities, near and far.

# References and Suggested Resources

Active - active.com

Amphipod Inc. - amphipod.com

B.O.B. Gear - bobgear.com

Body Glide LLC. - bodyglide.com

BUFF® - buffusa.com

Clif Bar & Company - clifbar.com

Due North® (Sure Foot Corporation Products) - duenorthproducts.com

Girls on the Run - girlsontherun.org

GU Energy - guenergy.com

Hammer Nutrition - hammernutrition.com

ICESPIKE™ - icespike.com

Implus LLC. – YakTrax - yaktrax.com

Kahtoola, Inc. - kahtoola.com

Medals4Mettle - medals4mettle.org

Medi-Dyne - medi-dyne.com

NATHAN - nathansports.com

Pet Gear Inc.® - petgearinc.com

Road Runners Club of America - rrca.org

Rodale Inc. - rodale.com

RunGuards LLC. - runguards.com

Runner's World - runnersworld.com

Running Blind - runningblind.org

Running in the USA - runningintheusa.com

Running USA - runningusa.org

Snowshoe Magazine - snowshoemag.com

Stretch to Win Institute - stretchtowin.com

Trail Runner Magazine - trailrunnermag.com

Ultimate Direction - ultimatedirection.com

UltraRunning Magazine - ultrarunning.com

United in Stride - unitedinstride.com

United States Association of Blind Athletes - usaba.org

United States Snowshoe Association - snowshoeracing.com

USA Masters Track & Field - usatfmasters.org

USATF Masters usatf.org/groups/Masters

USA Track & Field, Inc. - usatf.org

# About the Six-Word Lessons Series

Legend has it that Ernest Hemingway was challenged to write a story using only six words. He responded with the story, "For sale: baby shoes, never worn." The story tickles the imagination. Why were the shoes never worn? The answers are left up to the reader's imagination.

This style of writing has a number of aliases: postcard fiction, flash fiction, and micro fiction. Lonnie Pacelli was introduced to this concept in 2009 by a friend, and started thinking about how this extreme brevity could apply to today's communication culture of text messages, tweets and Facebook posts. He wrote the first book, *Six-Word Lessons for Project Managers*, then started helping other authors write and publish their own books in the series.

The books all have six-word chapters with six-word lesson titles, each followed by a one-page description. They can be written by entrepreneurs who want to promote their businesses, or anyone with a message to share.

See the entire *Six-Word Lessons Series* at
6wordlessons.com

Made in the USA
Lexington, KY
26 July 2017